Trish Elkins
A Love Story

Patricia Karpas

Acknowledgement

This little book, honoring Trish Elkins and her story, would not have been possible without both Trish and her beloved husband, Garrett Morrison. Their willingness to share what it's like to live with a devastating illness, with vulnerability and authenticity, has been a gift to many of us near and dear to them.

They allowed me into their lives through a series of interviews, but also as a dear friend, and, ultimately, like family. Their indelible imprint lives on in so many of the lives they have touched. Their humor and ability to love flawlessly (in good times and bad) has inspired me in immeasurable ways. Theirs is a relationship that has weathered the worst we might imagine, with grace and honesty. Even when they bicker, complain, spew frustration and are incredibly raw, the love they have for each other always wins out.

There are no words to express how grateful I am that these two humans have been in my life. I have immersed myself in every moment as Trish has shared her thoughts, feelings, emotions and challenges in our zoom interviews from 2020 to 2022.

I'm also grateful for my writing coach and collaborator, Marissa Handler. She's been instrumental in supporting me from start to finish. Her ability to find just the right words is truly a gift. She's a brilliant writer and a wonderful human.

My own writing journey has been kindled by my annual writing group and our retreats. We meet to support each other in our love of writing. Our group, Emily, Aislinn, Eileen, Jen and our writing teacher (and author), Todd... have pushed, challenged and motivated me to continue even as my inner critic dictates otherwise.

I love this group.

Dedication

This book is, of course, dedicated to Trish Elkins. My dear friend. The silly one who can laugh — and make me laugh — even as she suffers quietly.

"I wanted a perfect ending. Now I've learned the hard way that some poems don't rhyme, and some stories don't have a clear beginning, middle and end. Life is about not knowing, having to change, taking the moment and making the best of it, without knowing what's going to happen next. Delicious Ambiguity."

Gilda Radner

Contents

Introduction　　　7

Meeting Trish　　　10

Diagnosis　　　24

Love Story　　　39

Introduction

This book was born of a serendipitous friendship spurred on by a withering coleus plant I'd rescued in a dark, underground garage.

I met Trish in 2017, about a year before she was diagnosed with Corticobasal Syndrome, the devastating neurodegenerative illness inherited from her father. She was a healthy, strong, beautiful RN wearing green scrubs when I met her in the condo building where we both lived. The elevator made an unwelcome stop on the first floor just after I'd hit 4 on the elevator panel. Surprised to see someone, I rather randomly asked her if she'd like to help me with Ani, the weepy plant in my arms that I'd quickly named as I jumped on the elevator. Trish said yes.

This was our first exchange, an unexpected and fortuitous relationship that lasted about a year. It was perfect.

Neighbors are always asking neighbors for help.

But this? This was different.

What started as a plant co-parenting arrangement turned into a friendship that led to a series of interviews on zoom, during Covid, that explored the challenging feelings and experiences that inevitably accompany a debilitating, chronic and, likely, terminal disease. These interviews unleashed an abundance of emotions; a somewhat chaotic stew, told with a clarity and grace one rarely sees.

It's unusual to meet someone like Trish, infectious in her charm and affability, and so willing to open up and share her very real feelings, the good, bad, very bad and the unimaginable. And there were many of each. I hung on to every word she shared; relished in her ups and listened to the downs, as she communicated with elegance and ease, rattling between laughter and tears.

This book is based on these interviews and includes dialogue directly from Trish, some from Garrett, as well as my own observations. The interviews, and our friendship, has been concurrent with the progression of the illness that has robbed her of almost all movement at the time of this writing.

There were hundreds of pages of transcripts from our recordings. Not everything is included in this little book. I chose the stories that I felt captured the essence of Trish, and the essence of Trish and Garrett together. At the end of the day, this is a love story. A love story about these two amazing humans, but also, readers will easily notice how much I have grown to love Trish.

And while Trish can't move as she once could, Trish is still Trish. Inside. Milo, my quirky little dog sits on her lap, and he is not a lap dog. Her belly laughs make me howl harder than ever. Her sarcastic jokes and jabs remind me that you never lose your wit and sense of humor. I love this even when I'm the butt of her jokes. She loves to kid me about almost anything. And, I say to myself, thank you. Tease away. I'll treasure her forever.

She is a keeper.

Meeting Trish

'd noticed Trish long before we actually met. Probably everyone in our apartment building had. She was beautiful, her body toned like a runner, her eyes blue, her blondish hair falling perfectly past her shoulders. I'd see her walking around the gardens in her green scrubs and I'd wonder what her life was like. Young, professional, active, stunning. Always with a wide smile. Neighborly curiosity.

We met by luck. I'd just rescued a plant that I'd seen withering in our shared underground garage for four straight days and I finally felt a tug. I needed to rescue this plant though, sadly, I had no real skills to actually care for it. Regardless, I did grab it from the top of the jeep it was sitting on in a last ditch heroic effort. As I was reluctantly bringing it to my home on the fourth floor, the elevator stopped on the first floor. When the door opened I saw Trish standing there, with her smile and green scrubs.

"Will you co-parent this plant with me?" I blurted as I held it out in front of me.

Without a pause, she said yes. If she thought me or my bizarre outburst strange, she certainly didn't let on.

Butterscotch, I thought to myself. I use this word when someone seems unusually warm and inviting. She'll be perfect for Ani, the name I'd given the plant in our short time together.

I explained that Ani had been abandoned in the underground parking garage. Several days of watching it languish prompted me to pick it up. I tried to ignore the fact that plants rarely survive in my care. My slightly frenetic lifestyle as a media executive-turned-entrepreneur didn't give me the space to focus on such things as caring for plants, properly loading a dishwasher, tucking in the bedspread. I'd missed the basics. I did have a dog, though he sometimes had to run to the toilet and stare at it to remind me he needed water. But this plant...this was a rescue mission.

"You see, I just found it and I travel a lot, and would it be okay if I dropped it off at your door when I'm leaving town?"

We never talked about our co-parenting strategy. I would just drop Ani off at apartment 104 where, I later learned, Trish lived with her husband Garrett. When I was leaving town, I'd text Trish that Ani was at her door, adding a happy face emoji. And when I returned, I'd text her that I was back to pick Ani up. The relationship was blissfully simple.

Ani mostly thrived until I finally found a plant expert to take her, where she rather magically flourished. Then Trish and I simply went our separate ways. Trish later reminded me of the truth I'd overlooked. Ani just barely survived our care. None the less...she had a happy ending.

I didn't expect there would be more chapters to this story. But a year later, this happened:

I stepped out of my car in the underground garage to someone calling my name. It was Garrett. I didn't recognize him at first.

"Patricia! I sold you your Tiguan," he said, as I struggled to place him. Then I remembered him from the car dealership. He was hard to forget. Lanky, mid-thirties, with a toothy grin, Minnesota nice, honest and charming. He was the unlikeliest of salesmen, not pushy at all. I had bought my silver Tiguan mostly because, well, there was just something about him. Butterscotch.

We stood talking for a few minutes in front of the elevator. He shared with me that he wasn't working anymore because he needed to be home to care for his wife. I'm not sure exactly why he told me what he did next—perhaps he felt a neighborly connection, perhaps it was just his open nature.

"She has a neuro-degenerative disease," he said, still with a gentle smile. Then he mentioned her name. Trish.

"Really? Trish with the green scrubs?" I couldn't wrap my head around this. My Trish? I thought absurdly.

"Yes. Trish, the nurse." And, still as calm as if telling me he was on his way to Costco to buy almond butter, he told me she had inherited this likely terminal illness from her father.

I wished I had time to let this soak in, to formulate a response worthy of this news, as if such a thing were possible. Instead I said, "I have a meditation app. Would she like to learn meditation?"

He smiled. "Yes, I'm sure she'd like that." He didn't appear at all confused or bothered by my response, even though to me it seemed almost silly. He tells me his wife has a terminal illness and I offer my app.

I ran up to my apartment and immediately emailed her an annual promo code for the Meditation Studio app. I wanted to do more. Afterall, she was my co-parent.

So many people sign up for a meditation app with the intention of building a daily practice, but rapidly get distracted or lose interest.

Not Trish.

A few weeks later, a note was at my door.

Thanks,
you're outta this world!

Patricia!

Thank you so much for the meditation studio hook up! I've been using it for sleep every night, when I get a little down during the day, and Garrett & I listen to one each morning. You are amazing on there — very inspiring. Life has been hard this past year and these meditation have helped me so much. They help me focus on what I can do, rather than what I can no longer do. Thank you for your kindness, generosity, and support!
Much Love,
Trish + Garrett

She was using the app. Her neurologist had told her that meditation might be helpful, so she was open to giving it a try.

She would tell me she loved Chodo's throaty voice and Koshin's soulful breath meditations. She didn't like the accents from Australia and New Zealand, my favorites. She knew the names of many of the teachers and meditations and she'd share her opinions with me as she scouted through the tracks. She knew how to use all the features, and she was adding music and ambient sounds to the meditations she liked.

Breathe deep. Find your center. Accept what is. Be kind to yourself.

Her receptiveness and discipline surprised and delighted me. She'd tell me that there were very few medicines that were giving her any relief. But meditation was offering some comfort with the pain, sleep, and daily stressors. It wasn't magic, but it was helping.

I began to research her disease. It was impossible for me to imagine what it must be like to live with a condition that would rob her of the ability to move and possibly, to speak or even think. A condition that could neither be predicted nor reversed.

Her illness is called Corticobasal syndrome (CBS) and it is an extremely rare progressive neurological illness that falls within the overall category of frontotemporal lobar dementia, a group of neurodegenerative conditions. Its onset is typically at age 55 plus, though there is still so much that is not known about this illness.

The more I learned, the more awful it sounded. And the more I felt drawn to Trish.

We created the Meditation Studio app to help people with their messy lives. We would say "Life is Messy. Meditation Helps." I knew it wasn't a miracle cure, but it was a way to manage the mess, and in some cases, even transform it. But this?

These tools had certainly helped me with my stress, moods and, for sure, dealing with 30 years of corporate life. I was a seeker, always looking for new ways to understand and express difficult feelings. Painful curiosity, I like to say.

I often find myself wishing I were lighter, more like Trish before the disease. "I was always just happy," she said to me in one of our early conversations. "I loved my job as a nurse. I loved my boyfriend. I loved my life."

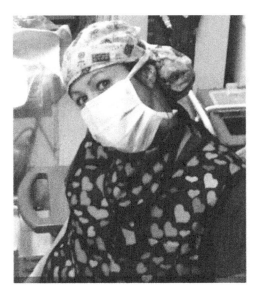

Simple. Light.

As I read about Trish's illness, I wondered just where our thread might lie. I felt a strong connection with her, although I wasn't sure what it meant. All I knew for sure was that I wanted to know her.

In January 2020, two months before Covid dropped its dark shroud on us, I began the UCLA mindfulness teacher training program. And while I'd created a meditation app and hosted a podcast on mindfulness, I'd never really taught anything, so I signed up to learn to teach, and in a way, Trish signed up with me. She'd been using the app for six months when I asked her if she wanted to learn more about meditation. "Yes," she said, instantly.

"Would you like to be my guinea pig as I go through this year-long program?" "Yes." Again without pause. Butterscotch.

And so we began.

In February, right before lockdown, she'd come to my apartment. In those earlier days, she could walk slowly to the elevator and ride up to the 4th floor, walk around the corner and knock on my door. We'd hug gently and sit down in two chairs I'd set up to face each other, and I'd lead her in a meditation. Afterwards, I'd ask her how she felt. And then; How was your week? And then; How is your life? And so we began our journey together, a series of conversations that filled my soul with the richness, authenticity and depth of her stories.

Mostly I just listened as she shared. I wanted to know what it felt like to be living in her body– a body that was inexorably growing more frail and rigid. How did she sit with the uncertainty of this illness? How did she cope with the constant pain? I listened. And when she left my apartment, I'd give her as strong a hug as I could without hurting her.

Many people have asked what drew me to Trish.

I can't say exactly. I just know that I entered her world as if, in the moments we spent together, it was the only world with real meaning. It felt like we were connecting from our souls, without the filter of the day to day busy-ness where most people spend their time. It was incredibly intimate, a kind of nourishment for the deepest part of me.

There was so much humanity beneath her stories.

As the reality of Covid sank in, Trish and I began using Zoom for our sessions. And as her story unfolded, I asked her if I could record. She said yes. Without a pause.

So I'd hit record and begin asking questions.

Tell me about your relationship, your family. What gives you joy? What overwhelms you? What was it like watching your father die? Your sister? How was it to get this diagnosis?

When she talked about her former self there was an air of confidence and strength. A light that shone from the inside out, as there still is today. Perhaps it's just more evident when the body is declining. Perhaps it's her ear to ear smile, her lively eyes, her belly laugh. Either way, in camera view, when only the top part of her body and her youthful face show, I see it. The nurse. The athlete. The yogi.

"I had no real worries, a great job, made enough money to afford everything I wanted and had this amazing guy that I could lean on for the first time in my life. I felt super lucky. When we found out about my likelihood of getting this, that became all I could think about. I don't know how to explain what it feels like to have your family 'picked off' one by one." Her face grows red, her eyes dull. "I mean, I worked as a nurse, sometimes with people who had dementia and I just thought, I hope to God I never end up that way."

I learned the word *perseverate* from Trish. I always used the word 'ruminate' to explain how my brain grabs on to a thought, repeats it, only to dig a groove so deep as to permanently etch it into my consciousness. This seems to only happen precisely when I'd prefer it not to. Anger. Regret. Shame. Blame. Like Velcro, these thoughts stick. I tend not to ruminate on happy moments, unfortunately. My brain chews on the things that I haven't quite worked out. Haven't yet found some universal truth to act as solvent.

Listening to Trish, I'd wonder how you stop perseverating when the stimulus is constantly present. The pain, uncertainty.

Over the course of these sessions her story unfolded. And somewhere along the way, in these deeply introspective and richly intimate conversations, I began to adore Trish. She was so honest and vulnerable, simultaneously frail and strong, floundering and pushing forward. It was all there, in this one struggling human.

Our sessions were often difficult, and Trish would be exhausted by the time we said goodbye. I often felt they should end sooner than they did. I didn't want her to feel drained. But she wanted to share.

I too felt drained, devastated for Trish, longing for a way to help her. There were many times I wanted to cry. At the end of each one or two hour session, I'd close the computer and simply sink into my couch.

I've tried to tell Trish the impact she's had on me, though I'm not sure she'll ever truly know. She landed smack in the middle of my world, and I believe this was no mistake. Now, almost two years since we started talking, I can honestly say that she's the best thing that's happened to me these last few years.

When I first saw the lonely little plant sitting on the hood of that Jeep, I had no idea why I felt drawn to it. No idea of the gift that Ani would ultimately bring into my life.

but I'm glad I listened to the tug, and that Ani led me to Trish. And Trish led me to a deeper understanding of what it means to be human, what we are capable of even—or perhaps especially—in the worst of times.

Perhaps every tug in the gut is ultimately a signpost pointing home.

Diagnosis

This is how you find out you're going to die early. And terribly.

When the results of the tests come in, the genetic counselor sets up a time for a call. They do not know the results, but in their hand is a sealed envelope, containing your fate. They aren't permitted to open it until they're on the phone with you.

Once you're on the phone, the counselor says, "I'm opening the envelope now." And then you wait.

"My heart was racing, I could hardly breathe," Trish tells me over Zoom.

"I heard her opening the envelope, and she paused and then said, 'The results are positive.'"

"And I'm sitting there in shock, though I'm not sure why. It's what I knew, what I expected. And then the counselor continues. "Do you have any questions?"

"What can you say?" Her voice drops. "I didn't have any questions because I knew there weren't any answers."

"I realized at that moment that I'd probably never work again. And the debilitating pain meant that my life would never be the same." Her face flushed, she looks away. "*Our* life would never be the same."

She shares this part of her story and I'm not supposed to solve, fix, or even respond. Just listen. Access compassion. "This sucks," I say. What I'm thinking is that there is no other response. It just sucks. And yes, I am aware this is a gross understatement.

Trish was born in Crowley, Louisiana to a 'very southern' family with five sisters and one brother. Lance, Skye, Jennifer, Lori, Robyn, Courtney. They'd play, bicker, and generally create chaos– dragging mud into the house, making fun of each other. Trish worried a lot and had headaches, but no one ever gave it much thought.

A few years later the family moved to Texas. Then in 1987 they moved again, this time to Littleton, Colorado, where they finally had a large enough house to fit the whole family. Her memories are of a very chaotic, but mostly healthy, family life.

Later, Trish trained as a nurse and went on to work in the ICU at the VA Hospital in Denver.

She loved being a nurse. She enjoyed science and biology and took a lot of classes in neurology. Her research paper was on a neurological illness called Pick's disease, a kind of dementia similar to Alzheimer's but far less common. It affects parts of the brain that control emotions, behavior, personality, and language. It's also a type of frontotemporal dementia (FTD).

When Trish was in her early twenties, her dad began to show signs of his illness, which in retrospect, ironically, looked similar to Pick's.

"My dad showed very odd signs in the beginning stages of his illness," she tells me, in one of our Zoom sessions. "Some we only saw in retrospect. He started to behave out of character, like he was a different person. He used to be reserved, strict, and quiet, and he didn't smile or laugh much. Sometimes he wouldn't say a word. We were always kind of afraid of him. My mom was the pushover and my dad, the disciplinarian. I remember a mostly happy childhood, but my parents didn't actually get along. My mom was always crying and my dad didn't seem to care. He was cold and emotionally stunted. Then seemingly overnight he became this joking guy that laughed and smiled and inappropriately made fun of people."

I've heard about behavior changes with some types of neurodegenerative illnesses and brain injuries, but never quite like this. His symptoms began to show just as he and Trish's mother decided to separate. Trish didn't have much detail on this, but it seemed that as his personality began changing, other things around him were shifting as well.

"He was 48 years old when the symptoms became noticeable. This is when he got his own apartment and left his job. Looking back, this seems strange as well. They thought about separating many times, but this was the first time he actually moved out. The only thing I remember hearing at the time is that 20% of his brain had been liquified. At first the doctors said it was Alzheimer's, because they didn't know what else to call it."

Trish shares the story of her family with great detail, and as if she's reviewed it thoroughly. She's not reaching for information. She looks directly at me through the camera.

"We weren't super close," she says. "He wasn't the kind of guy to ask us about our feelings and he didn't actually say anything when he left my mom and our family home."

Her parents ended up getting back together and moving to Louisiana with the hope that both their families would help care for him as he declined. Slowly he became incapacitated. As it turned out, their extended families had their own lives…jobs, kids, work etc., so couldn't be as helpful as originally hoped.

The stress of caring for her husband, along with complications with his entire family, caused Trish's mother to have a nervous breakdown. A woman who typically took fastidious care of herself and her house, she began to sleep all day long. There was mold in the bathtub. She stopped dying her hair and thought the devil was in the outlets. Eventually she checked into a psychiatric home, and Trish's father went to live with his parents.

When Trish's mother recovered, she took care of her husband again until he went into a nursing home.

He never really lost his memory, so Alzheimer's didn't seem likely, but there was no clear diagnosis for his behavioral symptoms at the time. He was in the nursing home for a few months before dying from pneumonia at age 52.

When he died, there was no autopsy ordered. "I guess my mom didn't think to do this. But this was what was later discovered to be frontotemporal lobar dementia (FTD). It was a terrible chapter in our lives," she continued. "But none of us thought anything more about it once it had passed. We just thought this was a thing that happened to him"

"We had no idea what was coming."

Trish's sister Jen was the first of the siblings to show signs.

It was her illness that led researchers to the clues that uncovered the characteristics of the gene that was indeed passed along from their father– who had obviously been misdiagnosed. Each sibling had a 50% chance of inheriting this gene mutation. And while it might appear in different parts of the brain, there was no way to predict where it would 'land' or when. All neurodegenerative diseases are partly caused by a build-up in proteins. Once the neurologists can detect where the particular proteins have accumulated, and observe and track symptoms, they can begin to understand what syndrome to expect. But there is still so much they don't know.

It was now 2015, and Jen was 37 years old. She had three young children. Her type of FTD was progressive primary aphasia— which meant she would lose the ability to communicate. As the disease progressed, it looked to the outside world like Jen had no voice or expression, no language or emotion. Eventually she just stared blankly into space, though it was unclear what, if anything, she could understand. She'd sometimes hit her hands on her thighs in utter frustration.

Jen's husband discovered that UCSF had a research study on this particular gene mutation. At UCSF they figured out that Jen had what her father likely had, and told the other siblings there was nothing they could do to reverse the path of this rogue gene. Jen died in 2018, 3 years after her diagnosis and 6 months after going into a nursing home.

When Jen died, most of the siblings agreed to be tested for the UCSF AllFTD Study. Only Trish and her brother Lance decided not to be tested, not to be part of the study. But none of them wanted to know the results of the genetic testing, which is what the genetic counselor advised. They knew their statistical chance of having the mutation and developing the disease, but that's all they knew.

It all seemed surreal to Trish as she grieved her sister and began to wonder about her own future.

The genetic testing conducted at UCSF revealed that a mutation in this gene caused the protein tau to build up in certain areas of the brain, creating what are called tangles, which would dictate the particular symptoms. These clumps of tangles are thought to cause loss of connection between the cells – synapses – and ultimately loss of the brain cells themselves. None of this is completely understood at the moment. Tau is in everyone's brain. It is only when it misfolds and forms these tangles that it causes problems.

But the researchers can somewhat predict how the disease might unfold, once they've found the exact location of the gene.

Since there was no certain expression or timing, the genetic counselor discouraged the siblings from getting the results. If the genetic counselor had, instead, told them to hear the results, would that have swayed their opinions? Trish wondered. Could they have planned their lives with more certainty if they were positive, or even felt some relief if the results were negative?

When I heard this, I wondered what I would do. Would I want to know? Would most people want to know, or would we prefer not to? Are we so suggestible that knowing would trigger an anguish that would slowly seep into our cells? Could this even spur the illness into existence? I usually like to know the endings to stories. I loathe surprises.

But on this, I have no idea.

Towards the end of 2018, just after Jen died, Trish began having some unusual symptoms. She noticed this at work as she began to have trouble doing some regular tasks. Her hand didn't move on command. Her balance was slightly askew. Occasionally she felt a bit robotic in her movement. Once the symptoms began, she became even more reticent of being tested. The symptoms seemed a little like MS (which her older sister had) so she began imagining that this might be it. Even hoping.

The alternative was unimaginable.

Her friends and colleagues at the VA hospital began noticing that her gait had changed, and that there were times she seemed out of balance. She was always a little clumsy, and they'd make fun of her, but this was different.

Then on a girls' trip in October, they noticed that she had trouble with some simple tasks, like getting her arm into her jacket or coming out of a pool. Her left hand moved slowly and seemed stifled when she tried to wave to someone. It was after that vacation that Trish decided to see a neurologist. He tested for MS. It was negative. When Trish told him about her sister and father, he said, "You have very good reason to be concerned."

When she said these eight words out loud, I tried to imagine what this must have been like for her. My chest tightened. I could feel a sense of the unimaginable being birthed, the ground beneath me slipping away.

You have very good reason to be concerned.

I'm back to wishing time would stop. What, if anything, could I say to her? Yes, this was probably one of the worst moments in her life. So far.

Trish did her own research, and that's when she realized that she might have a movement disorder associated with the tau protein and FTD. She became convinced it was Corticobasal Syndrome (CBS) after her colleague, Tracy, showed her an article about the illness. Her symptoms matched. At this point, another neurologist said to Trish "I hope to god that you're wrong. That you don't have this."

This is when she decided it was time for her to enter the UCSF ALLFTD research study where her sisters were enrolled.

It was early 2019. The researchers had great interest in Trish and her siblings, since it's such a rare hereditary gene, and because her family was so large.

The doctor agreed with Trish's self-diagnosis. He speculated that the tau protein was in the basal ganglia region of her brain, consistent with an expression of the inherited gene. It would indeed affect her movement. He was quite certain it was

Corticobasal Syndrome, even without the results of the genetic test at this point.

She didn't cry.

"I remember feeling like...God...I wish I had MS." On my computer screen, her face turns red. She continued. "And I thought to myself, who wishes they have MS? I knew from reading about CBS that it was terrible. Terrible. And I knew that nobody could tell me anything about the course it would take or how long I'd even be able to walk or talk."

I want to jump through the screen and hold her tight. I want to squeeze this nightmare illness right out of her. I ask her if she wants to take a break.

No, she says, and keeps talking.

Once all the rigorous testing is complete, the researchers, genetic counselors and doctors all gather in a family meeting, which at this session included Trish and Garrett. Trish already knew what to expect because they'd told her they'd be very surprised if the genetic test didn't reveal the gene. Everything they saw and tested led them to believe this. It was in this meeting that Garrett first heard the news directly from the neurologists. And while the actual test results wouldn't be confirmed for a few weeks, the team was in consensus.

Trish and Garrett, dazed by this new reality, walked around the city until they stumbled into a Chinese New Year parade. The frenetic festivities and celebration made the morning feel even more surreal.

"I was being a shithead," Trish said, "and he was trying his best to make things normal. But I needed to acknowledge this was actually happening and not be so normal." She took a breath, struggled to swallow. "And then, after the parade, as we took an uber to the airport for the flight back to Denver...I could see a tear rolling down his cheek."

When we love someone, we believe the reality we hope for will be the one that materializes until we discover that we have very little control over the course of things. Maybe sometimes.

I'm having a difficult time absorbing these gut-wrenching moments – and there are so many. There must be some cure or at least medicine for this illness, I keep thinking. I'm not alone. Garrett, eternally the optimist, wanted to believe this too.

When I began studying Buddhism in my thirties, hoping for some relief from, or at least understanding of, my complicated interior life, I balked at the emphasis on suffering, old age, sickness and death. This is a foundation of Buddhist philosophy. Everything we love will change and die at some point– unless we do first.

I once ran out of a lecture when they began talking about this. I pretended I was going to the restroom with a plan to duck out. As I was leaving, I heard the teacher say that, yes, we will, in fact, suffer– but we have control over our relationship with suffering. Pain is inevitable, suffering is not, he declared. That made a little more sense to me, but I still ran.

But as I grew older, and dealt with my first experiences of death, I began to accept this Buddhist philosophy. We do lose those dear to us. We do suffer.

And sometimes we even have a choice about how much we suffer.

Over the course of my conversations with Trish, it was the diagnosis and the accompanying mental and physical torment I struggled with most. I couldn't wring out any meaning from it. And when I asked Trish what meaning she makes of this, she said "none." This just blows. None the less, I've never seen anyone cope more gracefully.

In any single moment, I thought as I listened, someone is being born and someone is dying. And perhaps we're always dodging bullets in the interim. Is there a purpose to our suffering, I often wonder. Are there answers to our bigger 'why' questions? Or is the search for meaning simply an unnecessary distraction?

Love Story

I t was two weeks after their first date that Trish and Garrett talked about marriage.

That was also the first time they slept together.

They met on January 10th, 2015, at 7:07pm. Trish is very precise about the time when she recounts the date. They were set up by her ex– her best friends high school boyfriend–and his new wife. They'd sent

Trish a few photos of guys, and she selected the one of Garrett. And so it began. Trish drove to Boulder, parked outside Garrett's apartment and texted him to let him know she'd arrived. As she waited for him to come down, she didn't let herself get excited. She knew enough at this stage not to expect too much. Her palms were only a little sweaty. She also wasn't too excited about boulder at this moment.

And yet, as he got to her car, opened the door, jumped into the passenger side and said "hi" with his big, toothy smile, she had a tender knowing that something good was about to happen.

It's early in our conversations when Trish tells me about this. Only some parts of her body are rigid, and she still has movement. Her face is bright, eyes lit up, sweatshirt revealing one sun-bronzed shoulder as if to say, *I've still got it*. I look at her and I'm in awe of how beautiful she is.

The date felt effortless, as they moved from the most expensive restaurant in Boulder, Frasca, to the Outback Saloon, a fun dive bar. They were in jeans and it didn't matter that Frasca was a 3 course fixed price kind of place. They sat at the bar in front, chatting for hours, and never ventured into the dining room. No meal was necessary.

I begin wondering what it feels like to know that someone is 'your person' five seconds into meeting them.

I think back to my own first dates. Nope, never on the first date have I had that feeling. I've slept with some of them, but only because the mood was set, the wine was plentiful, and it seemed like the right thing to do.

I sneak in my own little thought about how lucky Trish is to have found her person.

I love seeing them together because I know that they're meant to be with each other, if such things are possible. And the more I see them--even later in her illness– the more I believe they're the luckiest people in the world.

I begin to think, as I listen to Trish tell her story and observe them together, perhaps their love bubble will rub off on me.

Cliche as it sounds, it feels to me like their souls are connected. It's the stuff of fairytales. And when I witness this, I forget their grief, and feel an unsettling envy and, also, a bit of bliss for them.

They met right around the time Jen was diagnosed, three years before Trish's diagnosis. When Trish explained the situation to Garrett, he was not deterred. "You have a 50% chance of getting hit by a bus walking across the street," he'd say. "It's not worth wasting your time or energy worrying about this." And then he'd look at her. "Trish, I'm not going to bail on you."

They married on March 7th, 2019 at 7:07 pm, precisely a month after her actual diagnosis. They walked to the county clerk's office in Boulder just as it was closing. "We had estimated that it was 7:07 when we met, so we wanted that on the marriage certificate," said Trish. Of course they did.

They had already moved in together, so getting married wasn't a giant leap. "I decided I loved Garrett more than I loved my favorite house in Denver," Trish tells me, with a grin, "so we bought the condo in Boulder, then, six months later, I sold my favorite house."

Had she not moved here– to the condo three floors below my own– we would not have our time together now. We would not have our year on Zoom–she under the siege of her illness, the rest of us under the siege of Covid. We would not have the relationship that has become an essential part of my life. I would not spend part of everyday thinking about her, wishing that she were free from this suffering.

When they were deciding on the condo, Trish would ask Garrett over and over, "Are you sure you want to buy this place with me? Because I could have this and if I do, it will fall on you to take care of me." And he would say, "If you're asking me if I'm going to leave you if you find out that you have this illness, the answer is no. I'm just not going to leave."

Garrett knocked down a wall and set up a cheery spot for her in the corner of their oversized closet, behind the bathroom, with decal flowers behind her and a table for her water. Her right hand, still able to move slowly, reaches for the water bottle and brings it to her lips.

"It's one thing to have the conversation when you have no symptoms," she continues, her eyes tearing up.

"Back then, when we talked about marriage and kids, he'd say 'Yes, I want to marry you someday, and no, I don't want kids.'" Trish was ambivalent about kids herself, so this was fine. "I think kids just stress him out, and he doesn't want the responsibility. He didn't even want a dog. He would say, 'I don't want something that's 100 times more work.'"

It is late December 2021 as I write this, and as the disease has progressed, Garrett has not bailed. Not even close. He is there in every moment. He puts cute t-shirts and pants on her tiny body, cooks vegan food for her, brings her water and smoothies. He helps her with her physical therapy sessions. He waits for her to fall asleep in case she has to go to the bathroom. No water after 7pm, please, he says. Many nights he stays up with her as she suffers through the pain and insomnia.

When we're all vaccinated, I can spend more time in person with Trish, but only when she feels okay-ish. When I visit, I see the full mountain art piece that Garrett carved and hung on the wall beside their bed. This I couldn't see from the Zoom window. There are painted flowers on the wall facing the bed, with long stems curving above the TV that plays music in the background.

Garrett leaves the front door unlocked so I can walk right in. Milo, my energetic puppy, runs straight to Garrett–who likes him, even as he hopes he doesn't shed on the couch or leave muddy paw prints on the floor. Garrett takes the bully stick and pretends to chew on it. Milo tilts his head, confused by this action, by this very silly man.

The bathroom in apartment 104 has been retrofitted to meet Trish's current needs. She can't move around without him. It's hard for her bare feet to grip the rug, and when she's wearing socks, she risks sliding on the cement floor. When we played Yahtzee in person to entertain my fifteen-year-old niece Ana while she was visiting, Trish couldn't move her hand to shake the dice. Garrett grabbed her wrist and shook it for her. We all laughed. Trish likes to laugh. Watching her laugh is my favorite thing. I know this is one reason everyone that knows her, loves her. Her UCSF Neurologist said she's infectious in the most delightful way, and always in his head as he tries to seek answers to these rare illnesses. Her family adores her. Her brother in law reminds her that she and Garrett are their favorite people. She's my favorite person, hands down. She and Garrett are just so darn lovable.

When I pop by, I usually find Trish sitting in her chair, next to the long silver bar where she does some PT exercises. She keeps a small pillow between the side of her body and her arm to help with the constant pain of her arm twisting inward, a particular symptom of Corticobasal Syndrome. Sometimes, like today, Garrett walks her into the living room area, seats her in the black swivel chair, and turns her towards me. The overhead lights are always dim, and the Christmas-looking sparkly lights on top of the kitchen cabinets shine softly. I find this soothing, along with the soft music that plays in the background. I know Trish would rather hear Natalie Merchant or The Gaslight Anthem, but Garrett has selected spa music. It's better for our conversations, he must think. Trish's face glows in the low light, even more than usual. I wonder if her feet need to be moved up onto the ottoman.

I give her the blue Ethiopian scarf that I brought back from my trip to visit my daughter Semira in Canada. The tag is still on. I ask if she wants me to take it off. "She likes to keep them on," Garrett interjects. "I do not," she says. He smiles. "Trish, you know you do that," he says, and she concedes. It's hard to know whether it's because she wants to keep the peace or because he's right. There's a speck of tension in the moment. I watch them together, the glances exchanged, the tones of their voices. Sometimes it's almost as if they are one person.

The other day I helped her with some PT exercises and, as we moved from the exercise bar to the bed–a mere two feet–I felt her slide from my arms. There is no option for her to catch herself anymore. Her body is stiff and unbalanced and her arms do not move in a way that can block her fall. Garrett heard us and ran to catch her. She weighs less than 100 pounds, but it's still too much for me; without him we both would have gone down. But I was startled and crushed at how easily it happened. And I knew what she was thinking. *Shit, I can't even move two feet on my own. Why do I even bother?*

Garrett moved her to lay on the bed, on her back, so we could continue with her exercises.

I'd have been crushed had Garrett not arrived in time to catch Trish.

When I see all that he does for her, knowing the extreme angst each of them is feeling, I want to put him on a pedestal. This man is a natural caregiver, a saint, I often think to myself. But even saints struggle. And I see this now as time passes. He doesn't complain, as he travels seamlessly from one chore to the next, but sometimes his tone is tight, his smile tired. "I'm the only one who can fully care for her," he tells me. "I can't leave her alone for too long."

As for Trish, of course she knows she needs help, but she wishes desperately that she didn't. She wakes up each morning wishing it was all a bad dream and she can jump out of bed, go to a yoga class, head to work, then run three miles.

She knows how lucky she is to have Garrett, but his constant presence is also a reminder of her decline. "I just want to go to the bathroom myself," she says, anguish on her face. "I hate this."

One day she couldn't make it to the bathroom in time. She can't move, let alone move fast enough if it's urgent. She can usually predict her timing and call Garrett, but not this time. She was shattered. But for a second they had a laugh. 'Now Milo is going to mark this spot,' said Garrett.

It's almost 2022 now, and there is a short period where Trish doesn't seem to want to talk as much. I'm hoping it's a very quick phase. She has this crazy idea that people are tired of hearing about her situation. Not me. I miss her when we don't talk as often.

But even when we don't talk, she's still very much a presence in my life, with sleep reports and emoji-filled texts almost every day. And when we do talk, she always wants to know what's going on with me. Recently I was away for the holidays, and she asked when exactly I was returning. I texted as I jumped into my ride. When I arrived at my door, there sat a jar filled with Garrett's homemade vegan 'nice cream' with chocolate and almond butter. They know I'm a ridiculous fan of almond butter. The card was beautiful, with teeny red hearts surrounding their names, each neatly outlined with black ink, and a giant handmade bow on top with perfectly-wrapped ribbons.

"Garrett was the first person I'd ever been with that knew how to take care of himself," Trish told me months earlier. "He was totally self-sufficient. So capable. He didn't need my help at all. I wasn't used to that and it made me feel more secure in life."

Secure.

Garrett is much more than capable these days. He draws colored hearts on holiday cards, prepares homemade vegan ice cream, retrofits the bathroom, cooks and serves dinner. He styles Trish's hair—sometimes into long, symmetrical braids, sometimes one or two buns perfectly situated on the crown of her head. Doing her hair has become as routine for Garrett as making a first cup of coffee. One night recently they invited me over, and had me lay on the floor, as Garrett turned off the lights. He then turned on his slide machine, which projects stars onto the ceiling, as he played his new sound bowls. It was magical.

So, yes, capable would be understatement.

"Before I was diagnosed, we fought about things like our different ideas of how clean the apartment needed to be. I'm neat, he's clean. There's a difference," Trish tells me.

A quandary.

"And there are just some things he gets intense about. He'll research things thoroughly and analyze them. And, if you have a laissez faire attitude, he just doesn't get it. He doesn't get how people can be super laid back about stuff. On the other hand, he's super laid back with certain things."

Clearly this was a puzzle she hadn't solved, nor did she feel too pestered by it. People rarely tell you the real details of their relationships, so these interviews seem like a front row seat into the best love story ever. Even when it's not at its best, it feels real to me.

"We don't bicker over those kinds of things anymore," Trish continues. "But even when we do fight, there is never a question of whether we love each other or not."

Awe.

As Trish's condition progresses, and as she becomes increasingly dependent on Garrett, she feels more like a child. Each time she shares this, she looks like a younger version of herself, so slight and tiny inside the Zoom window. She desperately wants to move on her own. Sometimes she does go too far. She fell seven times in one week this past Thanksgiving, got stitches in the emergency room, and ended up bruised all over. I wonder if these are mini-rebellions, governed by an urge to just do something, anything, for herself. I cringe when she shows me her injuries.

Garrett barks at her when she tries to do these things on her own. "I know he loves me, but it's really hard to be treated like a child," she says.

Earlier in my conversations with Trish, when Garrett dropped in, he would say taking care of Trish was no big deal. Not hard. And Trish would glance at me, roll her eyes and say, "This is nothing compared to what's coming."

These days, Garrett will tell me that he's the only one who can care for Trish, the only one who sees the real Trish.

When I interviewed one of the Neurologists from UCSF, he said they often spend time researching the caregiver as well, because the strain of care can be so high. They did a study where they could actually measure the stress of the caregiver and correlate this with the amount of atrophy in the patient's brain seen on an MRI.

Today Trish wants to share more about the sweet side of Garrett. This happens a lot, but mostly when there have been a number of very bad days in a row, and she's spent some time venting about his hovering. She wants to 'right the record.'

She tells me that she has a bad habit of going to bed angry and that he just won't do that. Whatever it is or has been, he'll apologize, and say, "It makes me sad to see you sad and to know that, even for a second, I'm the cause of that."

This man.

This is a rule I've heard before: Never go to bed angry, even if it means just touching your partner's toe to remind them you're there and this will pass.

Trish and Garrett have begun to look alike as their days become more fused, and as Trish's ability to go anywhere without great labor dwindles. Day by day he watches her, anticipates her need to stand up, sit down, turn around, walk over half-inch thresholds. Anything might be a barrier to her steadiness. He watches. She falls. Bruises. Bleeds. Feels defeated, again and again. He lovingly berates her for trying to put her clothes on by herself. And she longs for what is natural for the rest of us.

When she finally gets her first wheelchair, she's devastated. The idea of this is a crushing blow.

But when it's just a bad day, not a very bad day, she'll say something like, "I am everything to him and he is everything to me. I would not want to go through this with anyone else." Then she'll shake her head. "I am worried that it will destroy him. But he has a great way of bouncing back...and that's my hope for him.

And if I could only see one face for the rest of my life, be with one person by my side, it would be him."

Envy.

Then her face collapses.

"I want to put on lotion myself," she weeps. "I hate this."

Her emotions, and often our conversations, are a constant rollercoaster. I saw Garrett open the medication drawer one day and it was spilling over. Pain. Sleep. Anxiety. Depression. It's hard to tell how much of the rollercoaster is from the disease and how much is from these massive medication cocktails.

I ask them each one day why they think they have such a strong connection. They felt it when they met, so that's chemistry, I suppose. But I later learn that both of them lost their fathers when they were young adults, and this shared grief was a big connection as well.

I think about grief and loss often. About how it connects us, opens us to vulnerability, to intimacy.

I haven't asked Garrett how he thinks he'll grieve, but when I ask him how he makes sense of this happening in their lives, he tells me, "I just feel like something happens to everyone. It happens to all of us. Hers is the fucking worst and it's going to get worse. The only control we have over it is how we deal with it. I don't know if we can make sense of it. The only thing we know for sure is that we're born and we die. I've had a good life. Trish has had a good life."

And this from a man who isn't spiritual.

I wonder again where a love like this comes from. Karma. Good choices.

Trish tells me, "Marry someone you can talk to because in the end, that's all you have. Then she smiles and says, "I can't say I hope he marries again."

I laugh. Still, it's impossible for me to imagine these two people not together. I worry about Garrett. I worry about me, too. I will miss her terribly.

Our texts have become like love letters. *Hi sweetie… How did you sleep? How are you feeling?* She asks me questions too. She wants to know how I'm doing. She says, "I'm so sick of my own problems. It helps to think about something else." I share both my joys and sorrows, and she's graceful with both. She wants to hear about my travels and adventures, even as she continues to decline. I'm always torn, but her invitation to share is real. I imagine many people in her shoes would not want to be reminded of what they can no longer do. Not Trish. Her generous and loving soul rules the day.

This encourages me to open up to her in ways I don't do with others. On some level it feels like I have no choice. I've fallen under her spell. The more Trish shares with me, the more real she becomes. And the more real I become, in turn.

I suspect this is what we're all looking for– to be fully seen, to be loved despite our tender bits, our rough edges.

I like to call what Trish and Garrett have alchemy or magic.

But I believe the truth is actually more beautiful: that they are extraordinarily human, and wise enough to accept that in each other.

Made in the USA
Monee, IL
01 August 2022

10692940R00038